How to Make Love

First published in 2025 by Blue Diode Press
30 Lochend Road
Leith
Edinburgh EH6 8BS
www.bluediode.co.uk

© Annie Brechin

ISBN: 978-1-915108-34-0

Typesetting: Rob A. Mackenzie
text in Dante MT Pro

Cover art, design and typography: Annie Brechin, Rob A. Mackenzie

Diode logo design: Sam and Ian Alexander.

Printed and bound by Imprint Digital, Exeter, UK.
https://digital.imprint.co.uk

How to Make Love

Annie Brechin

BLUE DIODE PRESS
Edinburgh

CONTENTS

DUBAI

EDINBURGH

LONDON

The Best Lovers

don't want to marry, they don't want children
or to settle down. They lay you

on a mattress in a room full of mirrors
and turn the switch to pitch black.

They drive you to an orange grove
in October. They leave faint

blossom on your skin.

Years later you will see their photographs
in exhibitions and remember

how midday fell through their skylight
how they brewed you fresh coffee

how your fingers tore
their sheets apart and your back

arched like a question mark.

The Kill

Sky the shell lining pink of the underside of a thundercloud
turned inside out, the second before it rains. He turned
you on your belly in the moss and his hand dropped

like a hawk falling

as it sights prey. One finger, two – three to stretch you. Arch
your spine, lie back against his pulse, wonder how he finds the spot,

how the hawk finds the feeble beat of his intended's heart
from so many feet above the landscape and, a second later,
closes his jaw around it.

Madrigal

Dawn should break too soon for lovers –
it breaks on me alone. You've gathered
clothes and motored down the driveway

and still the darkness comes. While others
kiss and talk as if it mattered
I'm lying on my own – and though it

hurts I'll tell you not to worry
because I'm not the girl you're going to marry.

Purple Pants Postcard

With thanks to Tim Wells

I have owned three pairs
of purple pants. The first
were torn apart by the fumbling fingers
of a friend of my sister's;
the second said 'babycakes' on them
which amused my 17 year-old mind so much
I wore them till they fell apart
of their own accord.

The third pair I still own,
a lacy La Senza job.
Real woman's pants; you can imagine
some city gent taking them home in his pocket
too smug to even smell them, too arseholed
to send one lousy text
saying 'thanks
for a lovely evening'.

Bonds

Between the flowers and the passing hours
There should be a space to talk about
Sleeping in handcuffs, waking up

With your back on fire, in agony, not through
Arthritis, or a sporting injury, but courtesy
Of tarmac in the carpark the night before.

There should be a place to talk about
Carpet burns on your knees, and the time
You couldn't sit down for a week.

When the vampire bit your neck it was just
A question of passion, and how best
To mark you as possessed, how best

To mark your memory, to draw out
The time of you inside me. To turn brief
Thoughtless encounters into something

You'll never forget. Here's the first time
My lover shaved me, here's the original dirty
Picture, legs spread wide – in this messy

Temporary bedroom, loud the soft click
Of the closing of the door, where the
Only word that's needed is goodbye.

As Above, So Below

My flatmate is on the balcony with his lover.
I hear their voices as if through water.
The air is thick and sweet; it trembles,
As stars do when they stumble
In their courses and blind the sky
With a dizzying frantic fantasy.

I'm not really listening, so this could be fantasy,
But I believe that what he says is, he loves her;
When dawn comes, he will take the rose from the sky
And place it in a cup of water
By her bed so when she stumbles
From sleep and her breath trembles

The pale morning air, its petals will also tremble;
Proving it's real and not a fantasy
And she's no loose tumble,
He truly loves her;
Enough to rescue the bodies from the water,
Enough to bring down the sky.

But now it is only dusk. I
Watch the air tremble,
Made visible in the stirring folds, the deep ocean water
Curtains, blue like your favourite fantasy
And not the colour of my eyes. No, lover,
I won't stumble

Into those stagnant pools again, won't stumble
Into those same mistakes I
Put behind me. It is enough to be the lover
Of the world as she trembles,
Her gasps binding the elements: land to sea,
Air to soil to water –

To drift... To float as if on water.
To hear above, young voices tumble.
She peeks up from behind the fan of her hand to see
If she has caught the corner of his night-mask's eye.
Her world trembles
But of course he loves her, loves her!

Desire like rushing water blinds the sky.
They stumble together, tremble.
The world's the fantasy, the drowning lover.

You Don't Rise

You don't rise anymore at the smell of perfume about my wrists
Or lift your head when I speak, or turn down the sheets impatient for the night

You don't lift your pen from the sheet, let the ink spill and smudge
When I speak, or watch the kink in my knee when my dress twists

As I bend down to get the milk from the fridge. You don't see me anymore.
It is not that you are looking at someone else, you have simply turned away

And I don't know what to give you to make you turn back – or is it
A natural progression, nothing can be given – do you always turn away?

Should I even be trying to bring your eyes back to me? Is it selfish?
Is it unnecessary? You don't fold my clothes in the drawers with lavender any
                                                                longer,

You don't rise anymore at the smell of perfume about my wrists
Or lift your head when I speak, or turn down the sheets impatient for the night

From Raw

After talking to you on the phone, I went home and cooked
for the first time since we'd returned from France.

Months it had been, more than two of them. Watched
the onions green in the virgin oil, chopped courgettes

and threw them in. As a starter, I ripped a hunk of Camembert so strong
it made their arms seem puny

all those men

who told me I was beautiful when they didn't want me,
told me I was starving when they did.

Cliffdeath

Love is the worst kind of fall.
It knocks your teeth out.

Like the Homeric dead, you can't speak
'Til you've swallowed the blood.

But by mistake, you may swallow
A tooth chipping as well.

Then you can only choke
Like a muffled chain's clanking.

*

There's no steel in me any more;
It's been warped and twisted

By love. Now, brittle and fragile
As a buried bone, gnawed on by old worms –

Febrile and faint as a baby bird
Which won't live out its first week –

Oh, what have you done to me!
I'm sleeping in my tears.

The Surgeon

and so you have been taken out of me like a rib out of adam
adam never liked that damn rib anyway it hurt
it ached in the middle of the night when he was trying to wank
it tried to work its way up to his heart through the lungs
(this is an essay on suffocation) it wasn't
adam's damn fault and it wasn't his rib's either
it just did what it was supposed to do
until it was ripped from him by the one who designed it
like I who designed your love have torn you from me
to be a separate person no longer a part of me
eating the heart of me and the cliché
of the brain pan sizzling in the alcohol of your desire

I was never so happy the day you said you'd given up drinking
It was then I knew that I had never loved you

and adam lay back   pained and happy   sent eve out with the lamb
to order the world whilst he fucked himself
hand in the hole in his side
the original precursor of heaven

Sometime, Never

For Blair

Is it because we go home at night
with strangers? Some seed in us
that warns our parents how honour
is changed now. My mother at the
sink, elbows bent to the basin, doesn't
even think to ask how many men I've
slept with. Everything about you
hard in the dark, mouth and arms especially.
I was hoping and not hoping to ever
see you again. Both, really. With
my tongue in the flower of your ear.

Morning

The moon swagged low and heavy
The moon sullen and jaundiced as a blowfly peach –

To leave the room.
To leave it glib and confident
In a dense hum of sex and honeyed toast

To walk through the morning.
To walk through its skulked horizons,
battered grey battening down
dented branches, fractured rooftops

The sky cut cold from waiting
The sky scattered and buried as a china cup –

*

I have taken to building
pictures in the morning.

Here is a body,
blinded by skin and sheeting.

I don't know how the breaking
of all this is to be achieved.

*

The lamp is moon gold. The master dyer's indigo
halts abruptly at the angles
of its influence.

Nothing but a room
is permitted corners.

Stepping outside, burnt
branches oppose frost whiteness.

To walk through the jumble of smashed tiles –
To leave, bladeless on the ice rink –
To leave

Into the Woods

One day I will go into the woods

the wild woods, the deep woods.
There will be a hut beside a well,
a disused chapel
with oil lamps to light for the elder gods,
that shall be my simple ritual.

I will survive on honey oatcakes
and the sweet well water
with the occasional cheese or fig
left as a gift by the local people who never
show their faces, only their respect.

If a hunter wants to leave a hare for me,
I will pray for him for a week.
He knows this.
The hare is succulent roasted with herbs.

I will spend my days
acquainting myself with trees and the ribbons of vines
which bind them as families
and their heartbeats of squirrel feet
and the dull buzzing of insects in the heat

I'll rub the earth to uncover maps of roots
and delicate truffles.

I will build dens of woven branches
and leafy bowers for the wood children
leave them presents of carved
teacups and dolls' plates
so they will think that there is magic in the wood,
magic of smiling kindness

and there will be a child with me a wild child
perhaps a child of the wood or one of my body
I will teach her and show her
how to make honey oatcakes and draw well water
how to catch the leaves with a careful hand and
how to write a prayer for the hunter.

She will become strong, stronger than
all the trees of the forest together
ah, my wild wood daughter!
She will marry the stars
and wrap soft goats fleece around me in my later years.

*

But before all this I must
wander alone through glaring dark
city streets alone and also lonely
I must temper my strength through fierceness and sadness
a thousand tumbled mistakes
agonies missteps tripping on
pavestones and glass smash
cut hand sick mouth stupidities of want
in the dark round
loins of tunnels and tubes oh this city

no child no one circle of faces
flickering like a bad etching and everyone cared for lost leaving
even as you speak to them always
gone going depart apart
and you yourself running away
all the seconds that you
stand still.
The daily grind. Work. Job.
Put out of your mind everything

but what you're doing and what you need
but can never do. Suits, swivel chair.
This is not the sweet air.
You came here
for pain among other things but mostly for pain
to siphon yourself away until you are empty
of all but what the world is
newspaper print lining the dusty furnished room of the soul
the soul stick whisky bottles under the sofa and fag butts
stippling the wall and the lust-filled whore boy in the corner
and the presentation you should be giving on Tuesday
and the bleeping light on the answer machine
which is a message from your boss
begging you not to tell his wife anything

Look at the world in you.
It has pushed you out, you are empty of your own self.

Now.

Go into the woods.

PRAGUE

Translation in Glucose & Fructose

Some acts can't be undertaken accidentally,
like making love in a snowdrift
or stringing your sugarcane bow with honey-bees.

Kamadeva sets his sting into each couple,
smelling the night-flowering jasmine.
How they swell to open. Colour,

mauve particularly, is an irregular verb.
Not less so honey, the only grave-trinket
to exit the pyramids perfectly preserved

and inimical to synthesis. Like love
it has ungraspable essence. Like consciousness,
honey is a schiz, a cut or death.

It will fracture with ceaseless fervor.
The god shoulders his bow,
leaves the air satisfied by fragrant convulsion.

Fantasie: 5pm

Tell me, if my face was one single blooming rose
would you pluck from me my thorns?

Have the small elephants which were troubling you in your corridors
emigrated to grow their legs to stilts,

the better for the butterfly-men to harvest from them?
If only the juvenile pink unicorn could find

the keyhole with its tusk. But the box
is closed on all sides; its fourth wall is glass

and double-locked. The horses
with their laurel wreaths and round buttocks

carry tiny tornado conquistadors uncomplainingly.
Everyone miniscule and bronze

is seated with hat and book. If I
thought life was a dream maybe my dreams

would end up like this. Tiger-clawed,
fish-clawed. Levitating fruit.

I would make presidents from my wife's ass
and a press in the stomach of Venus.

Come on, we'd all like to know what goes on
in the belly of that tart. Time

is the only animal which if killed, dies more slowly.
Few people know Dali also made tapestry.

Wardrobes

For Millie

It is late and the park
is nearly closed but the dog
needs walking,

even though you are scared.
That rustling beneath the trees
could be squirrels,

or girls being raped,
or miniscule angels come
to scuffle in the gloom.

When was it you first
understood that angels have teeth
and text messages from old girlfriends

were sent to chase us from heaven?
But we keep on
baking bread and planning

to buy wardrobes.
We don't leave the dog
mournful in her kennel

because of our own fears
of rapists. We remember
that there are no angels,

that we are older
than we used to be,
but somehow that is ok.

When we fall,
we fall on the light side.
We try to forgive.

The Girl

your boyfriend wants to fuck
looks like a Barbie princess.

She is wearing that sugar pink dress
you wanted ever since you were six.

Her hair is straight and blonde.
Her smile is white and wide.

She has a horse, of course;
weekends she goes shopping in New York.

She's something in PR,
with a name like 'Felicity' or 'Dominica'.

Daddy got her the job
and she's just perfect for it.

Comment faire l'amour (How to make love)

I dream about the good sex,
the kind that makes you come
just from the memory.
A fuck so hard you wake up in the morning
with your pelvis bruised and tight.
C'est pas possible, he said,
but it was. Three days later I could
still feel him in my stomach like a fist.

+

Pas de bisous, merde...!
Croatia is not as beautiful as your cock.
In a bar above the strip in Split
frantically searching for allusions to Catullus
to justify this explicit want –
all I can think of is
with the stitches out of your lip
if it were you beside me drinking mojitos
we could finally, actually kiss.

+

Je peux plus me regler
Morning in the villa, the sun
zebra stripes through the shutters.
The breeze is brushing
the honey-coloured curtain the way
your fingers touched me after.
The one I should be thinking of
is in the next room working.
I touch myself and think of you.

+

J'ai plus de force
The sea here is so clear
I can see every rock and pebble.
Naked, underneath me.
Glittering.

I keep trying to purify myself
but the wrong things get washed away.
I'm left with your name, three nights
and the heat. Oh, the heat.

+

The sun is warm
like your palms.

The sea tastes slick and salt
like your sweat.

The pebbles digging into my shoulder
remind me of your teeth.

Merde.

+

Stop moving
he said, but I wish I hadn't.
I'm not letting you go, he said.
But he did. Out
from the wreckage of the hotel room
into the summer night heat.

The tram came too quickly,
rattling impatiently up.

Indifferent as to whether
we had time
to say goodbye.

PARIS

Turkish Salmon

was not, not even closely related, but
being with you it was alright. In any case,
I had the sea bass and your laughter
because "it's local so you have to try it".
That was the last night before we realised
we were completely broke. The next morning
we took a ferry to the island
where you'd hired a hotel room we weren't sure
we'd be able to pay. On the balcony at nighttime
drinking faux-champagne, eating olives
and kebabs I made you slow dance,
a Raki drunk shuffle to Chris Isaak. Love, you said,
that's the way you called me, and when
you called I answered, Love.

Marmotte & Tigrou

1

When I think of you we are in
the corridor where we first met
you are impossibly tall, taller
than you ever were again –
black-jacketed, one earphone dangling.
We are laughing helplessly
at the wreck of a hotel room.
Eating sauce Remy, kissing
at tramstops. We are staying
in Tom and Cecile's apartment
before I knew them. I have no panties
in the taxi and we are making love
on the Champs Elysees.
We are going to the theatre.
We are buying whipped cream
on a Sunday afternoon.
We are in Berlin, smoking shisha
and I leave poetry to come
and find you. We are dancing
in Dubai and they throw us out
for doing the lift from Dirty Dancing.
We are missing a plane,
and you take me to get cheesy bread.
I am meeting your friends.
I am meeting your family.
It is New Year, and you are
ridiculously sexy in a sparkly
miniskirt. We are watching
France-England in snowy Prague
and even though England win
I still do what you want me to.
We are in my studio, you say you like

how I cook English breakfast.
We are at Deauville and you say
you will never eat the chocolate Easter rabbit.
We are sipping Efes on a rooftop
with a view of the Blue Mosque.
On bikes going round the island
stopping at the monastery
to eat borek. We are on the balcony
with fake champagne
slow dancing for my birthday.
For your birthday we are fluo,
you in a thong and boa and I
can't stop laughing.
We are broke at the Foire du Trone,
you teach me to shoot for soft toys.
You are calling me at 6am
to tell me you love me.
We are sending whatsapp messages
that are just strings of kisses.
You are buying a last minute ticket
because three weeks is too long.
I am sending you a selfie with
a crazy grin. We are making snacks
for my goodbye party. We are dancing
at the Blind Eye. We are at Yes Burger
with Pete and Natalia at 8am.
You get another burger.
We are in the Morvan playing
a petanque tournoi. I'm sick
and you look after me.
We're eating tapas at La Pena,
eating raclette with Yann and Alix,
drinking in Village Michel.
You take me hunting, it reminds me
how much I miss the countryside.
We're looking at flats, going

to IKEA, buying a bed,
debating about a mattress.
We're frustrated with the owner.
He's an asshole and you
stick up for me. We're having
Christmas dinner, still surrounded
by cartons. We're at our cremailliere,
dancing til the neighbours tell us
to take off our shoes. We're playing pool
at the French Flair. We are at
Stade de France, it's my first ever
live international rugby match.
We are in the hospital
just before your operation
and the nurse nearly catches us.
When I think of you, we are having
one of those long lazy Sundays
where we lie on the sofa
eat pizza, make love and watch TV.

2

When you think of me we are having
a drunken argument.
Over and over, the same thing.
You versus a screaming harridan.
I'd be an idiot not to agree
it's not attractive.

3

I cannot make you love me.
All the poetry in the world
cannot make you love me,

or fight to be with me
or smile like a crazy person
because I walk through the door.
To fall back into love
is a flip even the hardiest
of high-wire acrobats will balk at.
So I cannot bring back
the sweet animal names
we used to joke between us.
And I cannot rescue our phantom twins
from their "if only" future,
place them back into my arms
where in my dreams my palms tingle
at the softness of their dark hair
and we watch their eyes first opening
one set brown, one green.

Incompatible

You know I miss you but you don't
want to know. You want to know
what's the latest score, who's playing next,
where your friends are clubbing tonight.
I want a house on a beach, a dog,
a toddler running across the sand dunes.
You want me to be happy as long
as it is far away from you.

DUBAI

Anniversary/Come Springtime

The man I love
is half a world away
and hasn't loved
me for a year

It's better
to make
a clean break

Like stamping
on the neck
of a duck

still flapping
from the shot

Why
d'you hunt
if not to kill?

You don't take
the duck
home on a leash

Stroke its
feathers as it
shivers
fearing the pot

Promise it
soft crusts
and ducklings
come springtime

The man I love
is half a world away
and hasn't loved
me for a year

And I am game meat
hung
for far too long

Letter From Isolation

"Wir jetzt allein ist, wird es lange bleiben" – Rainer Maria Rilke, Herbsstag

A sports bar where the live guitarist
at a pitch too loud for comfort
covers the songs of *ma jeunesse*.
In that language made mine through bitter suffering,
the marketing intern nervously asks my age.
He tells me I look younger and follows up
by asking if I'm wed. No. Boyfriend? No.
His surprise and worry almost match my own.
I am *toute seule*, I say, and can't stop
thinking about it all weekend.
                          Arturo
is *tout seul* in the mountains, except
for the wind and the cat. The wind he claims
he is exaggerating, which makes me wonder
about the cat. He calls me the Yellow Queen
because of my constant laundry mishaps. He tells me
he feels like an imposter. It's true in reality
I know no one called Arturo.
                       I feel like an imposter,
living the memories of someone else's life.
Once I had a cat that would sleep so trustingly
on my shoulder as I slept. I left him
as I leave everything, without looking back.

If I look back, parts of my life are burning
with a singular unquenchable fire.
Every movie is a redemption story
but I am well-schooled in truth. The phoenix
is a monstrous repetition who supplants
its own children with itself. If you asked me
to give up anything more, even one breath of wind
I couldn't do it.

National Flower

Desert rock in Jordan
Nabatean graffitti
two thousand years old
shows a simple oryx
the type that would become
their national animal –
though we didn't see one
and I've never seen
a black iris either
though one once
bloomed in my ear
it was in another
colder country, before
I first saw a desert
late night argument
threatened to
pack my suitcase
after too many slivovice
his hand came out
open? or with closed fist
I just remember
being suddenly
across the room
the bud implanted
the next day we went
down to the country
so no one saw it
swimming in the old
disused quarry
I thought I had
water in my ear
but no it was
those indigo petals
unfolding, deafening.

The Dream

where you rock up in some small town
somehow miraculously driving there
(even though you failed your test twice)
over hours of open highway
pine trees gliding through the back window

and you stay in a shabby motel
with a startling mom-and-pop charm
faded chintz somehow kept radiant
like the faded frizz of the owner's hair
(call me Mindy) is made a halo by her smile

and you eat at the cheap diner
(the only one in town) which has pie
that would make Agent Cooper wet his pants
and endless drip coffee seems to restore the soul
and despite vowing to stay only a week

you take a job as a waitress
in a gingham dress somehow cutesy
but also dignified doling out drip coffee
and that amazing pie to passing truckers
and the truculent townspeople

who to your amazement accept you as their own
their gruff love enveloping you like the crisp mountain air
and one day in walks a plaid shirt
the local bad boy made good
back to reconnect with the town he loves

and somehow miraculously he's staring at YOU
from under camel thick eyelashes
and after a week of scorching hot glances
he takes you to the drive in
feeds you burgers and milkshakes

like you are both seventeen again
(like this ever happened to you
when you were seventeen)
and he invites you up to his log cabin
that he built with his bare hands

and he gets his drinking under control
and he reconciles with his family
and you find a stray dog on the road
and you decide to keep it together –
that dream, this is the dream

you must kill.

For Castiel

You are an angel and I am no angel
but we both own the same trenchcoat
and the same overcomplicated desire
for oversimplified epitomes of masculinity.
When people ask me my favourite myth
I don't say Persephone and Hades but Destiel.
The angel falling for love and making
mistake after mistake, paying for it all
with pain and suffering and eventually
getting brozoned. But let's not be canon.
Let's imagine you did bathe together
in the cold pure rivers of purgatory.
My myth is the fanfic, hands and feathers
in the dark grasping and clutching.
Sweat on the back seat, so salt I can
taste it, as if I were you and finally
he was yours, yours, yours.

For Louis on his balcony, listening to jazz

Monaco sun
over impossible blue bay

If those moored yachts
were my vertebrae

you could run your fingertip down
them

No two seas own
the same colour

the mediterranean's got
a golden glint

like a pirate's tooth
Flash me that smile

Even my bone's marrow tenses
against your absence

restless tides pulled
to a distant moon

invisible in brilliant daylight

We Live In Water

Dubai is merpeople
in neon fringed bikinis

no tails required
slick-skinned revellers

flitting between pool and plage
to finish in chromy towers

where we swallow as much
as we swim in...

Don't tell me you don't want
our poolside passionfruit vodka

don't tell me you don't want
our beaches that turn to nightclubs

our limitless champagne brunch
I won't believe you

I never believed you
that's why I came

#fuckyourdatingapps

A man who'll feed me wine straight from his mouth
that's what I want. Fuck your dating apps

your Tinders, Bumbles and Happns
fuck these endless robotic profiles

"I like travelling sports and good food" who doesn't
fuck them and not in the good way

I do not want someone who's "just a regular guy
looking for his partner in crime" when he's never

approached anything criminal especially not
carpark sex on a Sunday night

A man with tarmac burns scarring his knees
that's what I want, a man who knows where to bite

so it stays ripe for days who'll lick
my armpit slurping in my scent

A man who isn't afraid to use two dildos at once
that's what I want, who checks at every step

are you ok? while taking me apart
A man who asks me what I want

and if I answer, to drown in pleasure
shipwrecks me every time.

Party postcards

There are so many things
about this fucked-up weekend
I've still to tell you

How I got headbutted
on the eye socket
during the boat party

How the crazy
Zimbabwean blonde
fought the Russian prostitutes

How I dreamt of you
in your bed but
with my sheets

you were so warm
the light spilled everywhere

Real World Valentine

You know that email that means you need to email
another twelve people before you'll understand
the content of the first email? I think I'll
give up I think I think I'll write a poem instead
hoopla! it's valentine's day something
so much more important for single people than couples
we agreed at lunch today over overpriced toasties
they toast every sandwich here everything is a toastie
they had muffins with tiny hearts on valentine's hearts
not real hearts not the blood milk moon that tramps
inside every woman churning monthly in globby chunks
when I think of red I think of what every woman thinks of
when we think of red and it's not muffins beurk
and for sure it's not flowers all these roses are just
menstrual for me and I know I'm not the only one and they all
have twelve fucking petals like those twelve fucking emails
I don't want this junk cluttering up my inbox
if you give me something for valentine's give me a poem or
give me a tampax when I'm scrounging hungrily
at the bottom of my handbag at next months' time I'll love you
I'll toast you for that.

In my newsfeed

there are photos of a supermoon over Chicago
which starts me thinking of all the places I've never been
like a. the moon and b. Chicago.
Six countries under my scope, my desk
looks over a fountain five thousand kilometres
from where I was born and still I
am looking to go further. Always away?
All I wanted was to abandon myself
to run away with somebody else, but the abandoned self
is stubborn, will not lie quiet in her cage.
She shakes, rattles the bars, she screams.
She gets out. She goes hitchhiking
by the long roads of summer, some cars stop,
some don't. She drinks whisky in bars.
She comes to find me saying what
on earth are you doing here, living
the good life with your mani-pedi.
Who is this man who thinks you are an object?
Whatever happened to the rough streets
of your philosophy?

Scratch me

Such an itch you are
man I don't quite know

all the things you might say
if we were on your terrace
with a beer

I see you've laid down
the astroturf
recollared the dog

what happens next
in this sun-watched
afternoon scene

at a given moment
am I also laid down

boneless
in my black sundress

how can I anticipate
the mysterious labour
of your tongue and lips

For my exes

I wish you happiness
I wish you green lights all the way home
Picnics that are never marred with rain
To know you've been loved and you will be again
May your father never fight with your mother
I wish you happiness, you and your brother
And your sister and all who share your name
I wish you fine whisky and rum
And now and again, on a big night out, cocaine
I wish you both stability and fun
Steady work and steady friendships
A job and people you can count on
I wish you fortitude
The strength I know is in you like a fund
I wish you bliss and peacefulness
And satisfaction when the day is done
Good movies, books that linger like a dream
Memories only of times when the sun shone
I wish you happiness
The certainty of knowing I was not the one
I wish you green lights all the way home.

EDINBURGH

Tainted Love

for Ed

When the smell of our shite mingles, that's amore.
Sitting on the chilly crapper inhaling deeply, remembering
that there is no worst of you only best.
I'm a sadluck fool but hearts are made to be opened.
Hearing you grunt as you lift from the bedroom
(the moss green bedroom whose paint scheme I stole
from another poet I admired too much) – that's amore.
Each huff, the panted numbers counting down.
I adore your body sore and backbroke striving for more.
When you scratch your balls while doing a jigsaw.
When you take the bins out. When I wash up.
Washed up on a shore of longing, all cuntlicked
so blissful I could burst, a sea urchin
flashing its spines out – isn't that the best ecstasy?
Everything you waste is my favourite perfume.
You said our love language is doing things for each other.
But mine's dirtier, down in the soil
where our excrement melds into a single unique soup.
Love, I would gild it if I could.

As I stuff the bloodied sheets into the washing machine

I wonder if you ever think you go too far
and think of all the times I've gone too far
like a bad Belle and Sebastian song
yet landed here with you, my beauty

gash on the forehead you refused to have stitched

that time I cheated and hid it, that time I cheated and told
to so many other men a lifetime ago
I still have the wedding menus in my emails
from all those bastards I was a bitch to

you don't envy their glazed melon and duck a l'orange

thank heaven it's only concussion
though our friends glance askance
your left eye flowering like the orchid I bought at Christmas
when we had no money for bread.

The Pianists' Pup

Sometimes the angelfish slipper into my gaze.
They shimmer like Liberace's jackets.
Bend down, hug me, then disappear.
Flitting and skittering, their notes a-jitter.

Mostly, I lie on the bed and have a hot water bottle
at my bum. I don't know the hot pink fluff,
seeing only moonshine, watch you scoff it.
You are all sparkles and ping-ping clipping.

I'm best at what you lot call squirls.
Run, run, Beryl! Do I falter at my name and fall back
or do I go faster? Little ball of moonlight
whiter than cornflour, powdered one.

I am loved at least, at last – and licked.

Birds on the Wire

For Chris C

Drunked out in Praha town with the boys, early days,
for me at least, and *dam si jeste jedno*
in Bukowski's as we downed them
sleek as swannecks.

Could have been Haight-Ashbury, '67, we were all
afizz with something, a driving ambition –
The ambition was poetry,
lofty as eaglewings.

Now, settled but never settling, saw you last
on a coffee terrace in the 'burg.
Sunshine smacked our heads
and our words rose like swifts in migration.

Will I ever write again, says the poet
like all poets, and gives himself
to the clean life and the hard work,
a nested robin.

But his red breast will bloom once more.

Red Jumper

An essay on rural puberty

Mum thought I'd opt for soberer plum
but it was the scarlet chenille I grasped and hauled up to the counter.
The world was small and I wanted to scream it.
Red as mouths it was, as the kissing lips I couldn't taste yet.
Red as valentine's roses bought as a cruel joke.
But I knew this red was my ally.
You wouldn't take me out of there sober.
You wouldn't take me off the moon of my delight.
My red monthlies, messyessence of woman, globby like braiding.
I was a flag my love I was armies.
All decided in an Ipswich shopping centre
Under strip lighting and smeared chrome. You sure?
she asked and I replied yes like Molly Bloom
flower of my own violent mountain
(years before I read Joyce).
And when I wore it I was outcaged, wild
like a puma on a suburban heath, the leash forgotten.
My soul itself red as a lover is in the dark.
What do you say, girl that was
who would leave the sober world behind for the circus
of wine and lovers? Did I match
your expectations?

The Sculpture

Some people carve happiness out of this world
like a sculptor carving a beautiful image
from wood, or stone. They leave behind
their father's landscaping business
and ride round Europe on a motorcycle
with their new wife. Thirty years later, still in Prague
and the walls pulsing with a new colour.
How do you make it all new, again and again?
Jim, you gifted me the best email of my life,
in which you told me I had and was the gift.
Please keep being you, one of the best men I know.
In winter nights I light a candle to remind myself
of all my friends' generosity. And you are there,
whittling away, getting to the heart of the shape
inside the shape which is your own true centre
pit and kernel that you chisel into wonder
over and over.

The Unexpected

They fed us fire whisky in the limousine
and we started kissing
your tongue small red and pointed
like a birds eye chilli

my Irish friend had never seen me with a girl

at the club you pulled me aside
and into the ladies
on my knees you slapped me
your taste like limes

mad beating heart saying yes risk this yes

nameless your tight skin
breasts like apples
you were all the fruit
rainbow on my lips

exit: dazed by night/our friends' unsure grins

peach of the desert
if I could find you again
I would let you bite into me
with your crazy eyes

New Revenge

Our fat bellies make sicksweet love.
This is the true revenge body –
not the skinnyslick limbs of Dubai's
golden sands, eating themselves
through months of yearning, sunbronzed
and yoga toning with as much substance
as a coke zero. No, this is
the cream and honey. This is
the yearned for obtained – squandered,
almost – but at the last minute
soothed with suckbright kisses.
Let me wobble, waddle – my breasts
pendulous as the bonehard moon,
my arse like a galleon in sail,
my belly – that belly – round
as a casserole of succulent meats.
Let me give you a ride on this mental go round.
Let me fuck you silly on a melt of pink.
We dovetail smooshy and collapse
to our own private glory of lux.

One Knee

Black rock shore.
White smoke rolling
Over red brown hills.

They're burning back the gorse
And we have come to the edge of the world
To find the comforts of wind farms and WiFi

And the curse of tourists like a virus,
A blight of which
We are undoubtedly part.

Your left hand
Steady on the wheel as
You drink hot tea with the right.

I'll put a ring on it.
And we'll drink red brown ale with singers
Who love cowboys and Springsteen.

Open water.
Vermilion postbox.
We have come to the edge of the world:

I love you.

Acknowledgements

...are due to the following publications in which some of these poems, or drafts of them, first appeared: Mildly Erotic Verse (The Emma Press), The Wolf, Rising, Obsessed With Pipework, Rakish Angel, B O D Y, Poetry Wales, Magma, Hinterland, London Grip, The Interpreter's House, bad lilies, fourteen poems, The High Window.

Notes

p. 30 **Fantasie: 5pm**:   stanza 9, line 2 – "press", in this context, is a word of Irish derivation meaning a cupboard or drawer.

p. 50 **National Flower**:   Iris *nigricans* is one of the national symbols of Jordan.

Annie Brechin received a Jerwood/Arvon Young Poets Apprenticeship in 2003 at the age of 19. After stints living, writing and performing in Prague, Paris and Dubai, she settled down in Edinburgh. Her debut full-length collection, *The Mouth of Eulalie,* was published by Blue Diode Press in 2022. *How to Make Love* is her second collection.